Whoopi Goldberg

FROM
STREET
TO
STARDOM

Whoopi Goldberg

FROM
STREET
TO
STARDOM

Mary Agnes Adams

Taking part BOOKS

DILLON PRESS
New York

Maxwell Macmillan Canada
Toronto

Maxwell Macmillan International
New York Oxford Singapore Sydney

Photo Credits

Front cover: Retna Pictures, Ltd. (Steve Granitz)

Back cover: Retna Pictures, Ltd. (Steve Granitz)

Retna Pictures, Ltd.: Michel Bourquard (2, 28); Steve Granitz (5, 6, 48, 59); Scott Weiner (10, 18, 46); Barry Talesnick (13, 25); Stills/Retna (15, 38, 41); Gary Czvekus (20); Busacca\Tisman (27); Theodore Wood (31); Walter McBride (32, 56); Joyce Silverstein (35); David Elkouby (43); Daniel Root (53)

Book design by Carol Matsuyama

Library of Congress Cataloging-in-Publication Data

Adams, Mary Agnes
    Whoopi Goldberg: from street to stardom / by Mary Agnes Adams. — 1st ed.
      p. cm. — (Taking part book)
    Includes index.
    Summary: A biography of the comedian and actress who won an Academy Award for her role in the movie *Ghost*.
    ISBN 0-87518-562-2
    1. Goldberg, Whoopi—Juvenile literature. 2. Comedians—United States—Biography—Juvenile literature. 3. Afro-American motion picture actors and actresses—United States—Biography—Juvenile literature. [1. Goldberg, Whoopi. 2. Comedians. 3. Actors and actresses. 4. Afro-Americans—Biography.] I. Title. II. Series.
PN2287.G578A63   1993
791.43'028'092—dc20
[B]   92-23766

Dillon Press
Macmillan Publishing Company
866 Third Avenue
New York, NY 10022

Maxwell Macmillan Canada, Inc.
1200 Eglinton Avenue East
Suite 200
Don Mills, Ontario M3C 3N1

Macmillan Publishing Company is part of the Maxwell Communication Group of Companies.

First edition

Printed in the United States of America

10 9 8 7 6 5 4 3 2 1

CONTENTS

Movin' On Up

It is very important for me to win the Academy Award. No black woman has ever had an Academy Award as Best Actress. Ever! And the last Academy Award that went to a black woman was for Best Supporting Actress, in 1939, to Hattie McDaniel in Gone with the Wind.

So I want one.

—Whoopi Goldberg

The sun, which some say burns a little brighter in Southern California, is just beginning to set behind the Hollywood Hills. Down below, at the entranceway to the Shrine Auditorium, men in tuxedos and women in sparkling gowns make their way past a wave of screaming fans.

The time is March 1991. The place is Los Angeles. The occasion is the annual awards ceremony of the Academy of Motion Picture Arts and Sciences. During the next three hours the most accomplished film actors and actresses in the world

A smiling Whoopi shows off her Oscar for Best Supporting Actress.

7

will wait, breathlessly, in hopes of receiving the most coveted award in all film history: the Oscar.

Policemen hold back the crowds so the celebrities can get through. People who have been waiting in the makeshift bleachers since dawn call out to their favorite stars as they emerge from the luxurious stretch limousines that line the curb. The name they seem to be calling the most this afternoon doesn't sound like a name at all; it sounds like a cheer. "Whoopi!" bellow the crowds. "Whoopi, we love you! Whoopi! Good luck!" Making her way up the red-carpeted walkway is the object of their excitement: Whoopi Goldberg, comedian, actress, social activist, mother, and grandmother.

Today, however, she's here as an Oscar nominee. Whoopi has been recognized for her performance in the 1990 box-office smash *Ghost*. In the film, Whoopi portrays a character named Oda Mae Brown, a psychic who helps capture a greedy murderer. She's up for Best Supporting Actress.

Whoopi waves to the crowd. She's done this before. In 1986 Whoopi was nominated for Best Actress for her part in the Steven Spielberg film *The Color Purple*.

She did not win.

Tonight, however, she and the crowd seem to feel that luck is on her side. Whoopi springs across the walkway and into the pavilion. Just hours later, Whoopi is holding the twinkling gold statuette. She is the first black woman in more than 60 years to win an Oscar.

From the glittering stage, she addresses the crowd. "I just want to say that this is going to a former welfare mother," she says, holding the award aloft. "If I can do this, anyone can. I thank all the people in New York who helped me through."

The audience cheers. But for Whoopi, the Oscar means more than a good performance in *Ghost*. It means that she has beaten the odds.

Because what many in the audience don't know is that living on public assistance was not the only challenge for Whoopi Goldberg. Growing up in a New York City housing project, she faced the challenges of dyslexia, drugs, divorce, single motherhood, and poverty—all before the age of 20.

For Whoopi Goldberg, the Oscar also might well mean "Never give up."

CHAPTER TWO

Life in the Projects

I knew before I was born that I wanted to act. I'm sure that my first conscious thought was "Where's the lights?"

—Whoopi Goldberg

If you closed your eyes you could probably draw from memory a picture of Whoopi Goldberg. She's often wearing dreadlocks and round gold glasses, her wide smile highlighting her high cheekbones. Her laugh is low and ready. Her voice is deep. And she always looks as if at any moment she will transform herself into one of her many comedic roles.

Most people can draw this image because Whoopi is everywhere. One minute she's on TV in a public-service announcement, telling us to say no to drugs. Flip the channel and she's hosting the 1992 Grammy awards. Hit the remote control again and she's Hot Rod Brown in the "Tales from the Whoop" special on Nickelodeon. And don't forget the five

Whoopi's trademark: round glasses and dreadlocks make her unforgettable.

Home Box Office (HBO) "Comic Relief" comedy specials, in which Whoopi joins comedians Robin Williams and Billy Crystal to raise money for the homeless. And there is "Star Trek: The Next Generation." In that TV drama, Whoopi plays Guinan, a friend and advisor to everyone on the ship. You have to look closely to see that it is her: Instead of her trademark jeans and sneakers, Whoopi wears flowing robes and a hat that looks like a flying saucer.

In all images of Whoopi, one thing is clear: Whoopi's a good sport. In fact, some would say Whoopi will do *anything* for a photograph. To the horror of her publicist, Whoopi once removed her dental retainer to mug, gap-toothed, for a photographer from *People* magazine. Another time Whoopi showed off her favorite tie-dyed socks.

Still another time, Whoopi discarded all her clothes and climbed into a bathtub full of milk. Looking like some crazy gargoyle, she sank under until just her legs and hair were showing—smiling the whole while, as if bathing in milk were something a normal person did every day.

What was this woman like as a child? What did she look like?

Whoopi laughs it up with Comic Relief co-stars Robin Williams and Billy Crystal.

What kind of childhood did she have? "[My childhood] was pretty good," she told ABC anchorwoman Barbara Walters during a March 1991 interview that aired just hours before she won the Oscar. "Kinda lonesome in a way. I had different interests from most of the people I grew up with. Kinda odd."

Motioning to her face, she said, " 'Cause I've always looked like this. Except now I'm taller. But this was always the face."

She wasn't the head of the clique, either. By her own account, Whoopi was "not particularly very hip." She admitted to Walters that the kids in her Manhattan neighborhood "could dupe me really easily."

One reason she was an easy target was the way she spoke. Most of the neighborhood kids spoke in rough "city talk," dropping their *ings* and *rs* and cursing. In contrast, Whoopi and her brother imitated the precise, polite diction of their mother. "When people spoke to us," Whoopi said, changing her voice to a high, delicate tone, "we spoke like this. Kids would say 'Wanna do sumpin'?' and we'd say 'No, thank you.'"

Naturally, speaking like Mary Poppins didn't go over well on the street corner. But it gave the young comedian her first lessons in dealing with hecklers. And, like any good comedian, she gave it back. How? "I learned to use double-speak," she told comedian Alan King in a TV interview. "I'd talk one way with my mother and one way with the other kids." Whoopi didn't

Shy as a child, Whoopi was not always the fast-talking comedian she is today.

know it at the time, but this ability to imitate voices and to change from one voice to another would prove to be her most valuable acting talent.

Looks and speech aside, Whoopi was different from the neighborhood gang in her resolve to be a famous actress.

"I started acting the moment I got into this world!" Whoopi once exclaimed. "I was born with my thumb in my mouth, hamming it up for the doctor." At birth, however, and in children's theater, the young performer was not known by her stage name, Whoopi. Instead everyone called her by her given name, Karen Johnson. Whoopi would come much later.

While still in elementary school, Karen Johnson appeared at the Helena Rubinstein Children's Theater and at the Children's Program at the Hudson Guild.

The Hudson Guild, in particular, had a great effect on Whoopi's life. She spent many hours there, not only because her mother, Emma, worked there, but because of the many things she could do there. Later, when Whoopi became rich and famous, she would talk about the importance of supporting places like the Hudson Guild.

What was the Guild? Then, as now, the Hudson Guild was a privately funded, nonprofit community center that gave inner-city children a place to play and to learn. Comprised of a group of buildings and playgrounds clustered in a crowded section of Manhattan called Chelsea, the Hudson Guild offered something for everyone.

For kids, it was a safe place to hang out. Besides the children's theater, there were day camps and organized sports. Best of all, the Hudson Guild owned a 500 acre farm in New Jersey, where there was a petting zoo.

For kids like Whoopi, who grew up in a housing project nearby, the Guild was a perfect chance to escape their hot apartments. One day Whoopi and the other kids might put together a play. Another day they might play dodge ball in the park. Still another day they might board a bus to the Guild farm.

For adults—especially single mothers and teenagers—the Hudson Guild offered an opportunity to learn practical skills that would help them find a place in the working world. It gave them job information. It helped them finish high school. It provided day care for their children.

Whoopi has not forgotten her years on welfare, and still volunteers to help homeless young people.

The Guild helped other people, too. It organized activities for elderly people. It helped families find and stay in new apartments. It gave counseling to families who were unhappy. It offered health care and advice to people who had experienced crime or trauma. Best of all, it helped neighborhood residents get to know their neighbors.

To the young Whoopi, programs like this seemed far, far away. Who was Whoopi to worry about the Guild's programs for adults?

But little did she know how much she would come to need such social programs. Because for young Whoopi, adulthood was closer than she thought.

The Hard Years

Even the down times were necessary for me. Even the bad times were productive. In order to make a living I did everything from being a typist to being a secretary. But eventually, it all served the purpose of acting.

—Whoopi Goldberg

By the time Whoopi reached her midteens, her life had changed dramatically. By 14 she had begun using drugs and alcohol regularly. By 17 she had dropped out of high school. By 18 she was married. By 19 she was the mother of a baby girl. By 20 she had divorced her husband and had no job, no skills, and no means of supporting her baby.

How did this happen?

Whoopi doesn't seem to know herself. All she knows is that there was a period in her life in which, suddenly, nothing was working.

The problems started in high school, when Whoopi realized

Whoopi's face reflects some of the hard times she spent fighting drugs and alcohol.

that she was unable to understand her lessons. When she tried to read, the letters did not connect into words. Worse, the words, when legible, did not connect into sentences with meaning.

School officials labeled her "retarded" (the word then used to describe what are now called "special needs" children). She was told she was "retarded" so frequently that she began to believe it herself. As she recalled bitterly to *Ebony* magazine, "You don't want to be *retarded* all your life. I was *retarded* for a good part of mine, and I just couldn't handle it."

Discouraged, she left school.

Years later, Whoopi would discover she had dyslexia, a reading disorder. But because in the late 1960s dyslexia was not as widely known as it is today, Whoopi was given any label that would seem to explain her problems—in this case, "retarded."

Now that she was skipping school, Whoopi had much time on her hands. Filling it was easy enough: She started taking drugs. Before long she was a heroin addict, a junkie. By night she'd do drugs, by day she'd find herself sleeping in Central Park and hanging out with other drug users. Though only blocks from the old playgrounds of the Hudson Guild, her new world was a thousand miles away.

When interviewer Barbara Walters asked her why she'd turned to drugs, Whoopi replied that "it was the 1960s," when many people did drugs without thinking of the consequences.

"So what do you say to your daughter if she says 'Well, *you* did drugs'?" Walters asked.

"I say," Whoopi responds with deep feeling, "that I was one of the lucky few [who escaped]. You can't do what I did then, today. You can't."

Or, as she told *Ebony*, "I tell kids, 'Save the money and just kill yourself because [if you're using drugs] that's what you're doing.'"

Many of the people Whoopi did drugs with are now dead.

Finally, at 17, Whoopi went into drug rehabilitation. For a while, things seemed to look up. That year she met and married her drug counselor.

When Whoopi was 19 she gave birth to a baby girl, whom she named Alexandrea. But by that time her marriage had dissolved, and she was jobless.

Whoopi Goldberg FROM STREET TO STARDOM

By now it was 1974. Exhausted from the rigors of New York and wanting to get away from bad memories, Whoopi decided to take an entirely new direction in her life. She went West.

She landed in San Diego, where she searched for an opportunity to act. Eventually she appeared in the San Diego Repertory Theatre's production of Bertolt Brecht's *Mother Courage* and Marsha Norman's *Getting Out*. She joined an improvisational comedy group called Spontaneous Combustion.

Money was still tight, and Whoopi had her baby to think of. To add to her bank account, Whoopi had to take any job she could get—and some of them were pretty odd. For example, she once worked as a bricklayer. When that job ended, she used her skills as a licensed beautician to make up corpses in a funeral parlor.

That's right: She applied makeup, arranged clothing, and cared for the hair of dead people being prepared for burial. Whoopi didn't mind ("If they didn't like the makeup, it's not as if they could complain," she says, joking.) but she was not comfortable enough to maintain the occupation as a career.

Whoopi is determined to help her daughter avoid some of the troubles she went through as a young woman.

No matter how many odd jobs Whoopi was willing to take, however, she could not stretch her paycheck.

She had to go on welfare. To Whoopi it was a loathsome, but unavoidable, decision. To this day she recalls the indignity she felt when being visited by a caseworker. From the moment she went on welfare, she longed to get off it.

Meanwhile, Whoopi followed the acting jobs. She moved to the San Francisco Bay area and joined the Blake Street Hawkeyes Theater in Berkeley. Moving into solo performances, she created "The Spook Show," which first played San Francisco and then toured the United States and Europe.

During her stay in California "Karen Johnson" became "Whoopi Goldberg." How did the name evolve? "Well," she told Alan King, "I am flatulent. And I have no problem just lettin' go when I have to . . . let go. So I got the nickname 'Whoopi Cushion' because that's what I sounded like, that rubber toy pillow."

To "Whoopi" she added the last name "Cushion," which she then changed to "Cushon," to sound like a fake French name.

But Whoopi's mother told her she should take a more

Whoopi as Fontaine, one of the many characters she has developed over the years.

Whoopi perfected her comedic skills by performing wherever she could find an audience.

recognizable last name so people would take her more seriously.

"Whoopi Goldberg" it was.

Not long afterward, Whoopi got herself off welfare. "The *greatest* thing I was ever able to do was give a welfare check back," she remarked proudly.

As Whoopi Goldberg, she took her act to a performance space in New York City called the Dance Theater Workshop. One of the people who attended the show was a man named Mike Nichols. A well-known director of such Oscar-winning films as *The Graduate*, Nichols had also done comedy. In the 1960s he and folk singer Elaine May performed on stage. Nichols was always looking for new talent, and he regularly attended the theater to find new stars.

Whoopi didn't know it, but this was her big chance.

As usual, she performed her evening of original material. Most of the stage characters were those she had developed while on her own in San Francisco. In her many performances, she had honed her characters to the point of true drama—a fact that was not lost on Nichols. The characters included a

California Valley girl who talks in surfer slang; a nine-year-old black girl who wants to take a bath in Clorox so she'll be white; and Fontaine, a recovered male junkie who looks at the state of the world and keeps asking himself and the audience why he went off drugs if things were so crazy.

When she finished, Mike Nichols came backstage and said, "You are wonderful. Your performance was so touching it made me cry."

On the spot, he offered to produce her in a one-woman Broadway show.

Said Whoopi, "I thought, what's the worst that could happen? If it doesn't work, so what? I've hit Broadway."

Whoopi was on her way.

One of the many faces of Whoopi Goldberg

The First Taste of Fame

Comedy lies in verbalizing what most people think but don't dare say. So you say it for them. And they laugh because they're telling themselves "I know just what you mean!"

—Whoopi Goldberg

Whoopi's Broadway show was so successful it eventually became an HBO special called "Whoopi Goldberg: Direct from Broadway."

Still spinning from her new fame, Whoopi was to succeed again, this time with director Steven Spielberg. Spielberg was riding his own wave of fame, after his hit movies *E.T.* and *Raiders of the Lost Ark*.

The two were fated to meet.

In 1985, just after Whoopi's show, Spielberg was developing a movie much different from his other films. He was making an adaptation of Alice Walker's novel *The Color Purple*,

Director Steven Spielberg gave Whoopi her first movie role in his film version of Alice Walker's novel The Color Purple.

which is about the struggles of black women in American society.

Spielberg needed someone to play the role of Celie, a woman abused by her husband. Would Whoopi be right for the part?

Spielberg did not know. He had seen many of Whoopi's performances and was impressed with her comedic talents. But how well could she do in a dramatic role?

He called Whoopi for an audition. After the first few words he did not need to hear more. He had his Celie.

The movie debuted in 1985. Whoopi turned in an astounding performance, matched only by those of such co-stars as Oprah Winfrey and Rae Dawn Chong.

The movie launched Whoopi's film career. This was *real* fame. Now Whoopi was known not just in San Francisco but all over the country. She got more and more fan letters. People stopped Whoopie on the street and started performing parts of the actress's *own* routines for her.

Fame was fun. But if it made some aspects of her life (like money) better, it made other parts of her life worse.

Whoopi signs autographs for her fans.

For the first time in her life, Whoopi didn't know who her friends were. The transition from semi-known to well-known was difficult.

To try to remain "normal," she kept her apartment in the Bay area and continued seeing her old friends from the Hawkeyes comedy group. As she said at the time, "San Francisco is the place where I know people will say 'Hey, don't get Hollywood with me: I remember when I had to drive you to the welfare office.' I depend on my friends to keep my ego in check."

New fame also meant that Whoopi Goldberg was not simply a person but Whoopi Goldberg, Incorporated. Whoopi wasn't her own entity anymore. Not only were there new friends but people who always wanted her time: newspapers, magazines, talk-show hosts, potential biographers. It was not long before she was surrounded by press agents, publicists, and consultants. When Mike Ovitz, one of the biggest agents in Hollywood, formed his Creative Artists Agency, Whoopi was one of the first performers he signed.

And everyone wanted to tell her what she could and could

not do. So many people wanted to talk with her and be with her that Whoopi had to struggle hard just to remember who she was in the first place.

Fame, she learned, was indeed fickle.

CHAPTER FIVE

Fickle Fame

If something [is awful, it's awful] because I wrote it. If it dies, it will die in my arms. If it's brilliant, I'm gonna take the credit. It's mine, and nobody can touch it.
—Whoopi Goldberg

While she did not win the Oscar, *The Color Purple* did earn Whoopi the 1985 Golden Globe Award for Best Performance by an Actress in a Dramatic Motion Picture. It also garnered her the Image Award for Best Actress in a Motion Picture from the National Association for the Advancement of Colored People (NAACP). That same year, the record album of her Broadway show won a Grammy award as Best Comedy Recording of the Year.

From this one would think that Whoopi would step right into another Oscar-nominated leading role.

Not so. Whoopi got starring roles all right, but none that earned as much critical praise as *The Color Purple*. Even if such

After The Color Purple, *Whoopi was offered parts in many movies and television shows.*

films as *Jumpin' Jack Flash, Fatal Beauty, Clara's Heart*, and *Burglar* did well at the box office, they were not free from critics' barbs. Media pundits crowed that her career was plummeting—despite an Emmy-award-winning appearance on television's "Moonlighting" and the well-written but short-lived TV sitcom "Bagdad Cafe" with Jean Stapleton.

To Whoopi, it just wasn't fair. When she switched from stand-up comedy to movies, people criticized her for not staying in comedy. When she switched from movies to television, people criticized her for not staying in movies. Exasperated, Whoopi finally addressed the issue during an interview with Alan King in 1991. Pretending her critics were in the room, Whoopi asked them, "Excuse me, do you have a *Color Purple* to give me? If not, and if you're not going to marry me and pay my rent, please go away."

Sadly, this was just another part of fame. Whoopi told King, "I take it for granted that people are going to give me a hard time just because I refuse to be what I'm supposed to be."

During this time in her life, Whoopi had to develop an even tougher shell than the one she'd developed as a city kid.

40

Whoopi shares a scene with actress Jean Stapleton in the television show Bagdad Cafe.

"Hollywood can really make you feel insecure," she told Barbara Walters. "It's difficult. First they'll tell you 'Oh, you're great. Just if you could change this one thing about yourself.' Then they'll say 'Uh, we love the way you look, but could you look a little bit more like this?' And then they'll say 'You're so funny, but don't be so strong.'

"Or 'That's not good, what you wrote—let me change it.'"

Her professional life was not the only thing in upheaval.

In 1988 Whoopi divorced the man she'd married in 1986, Dutch cameraman David Claessen. The divorce was bitter. Whoopi and Claessen fought over property and money.

In 1990 Whoopi's unmarried 15-year-old daughter, Alex, announced to Whoopi that she was pregnant. For Whoopi, herself once a single mother, this was a complex problem. Whoopi did not know how to advise her daughter.

Alex wanted to have the baby.

And Whoopi, who for years had preached the necessity and the power of personal choice, knew that only her daughter could decide. Whoopi told Alex that she would do all she could to support her and the baby. As far as Whoopi was concerned, there would be three mothers: Alex, Whoopi, and Whoopi's mother, Emma Johnson. The most important part, Whoopi told Barbara Walters, was telling the truth. "I'm glad Al felt comfortable enough to tell me. To say to me first, 'I'm pregnant.' Because it's tough."

Whoopi takes a drive with her daughter and her husband before their divorce.

The situation was especially poignant for Whoopi because to this day she says she feels a certain amount of guilt at working on her career while raising Alex. "I wanted to be in movies and do the things I've gotten to do. [Success] came to me on a silver platter. Handed to me. I got a shot and I took it. A lot of people paid the price for it. But nobody more than my kid.”

The pregnancy incident is reflected in one of Whoopi’s comedy routines. This is how Whoopi’s most famous female character, a teenage California surfer girl, recalls a date:

> *So, like, I go like, to the party and like, he says, let’s go for a walk, and like we go for this really amazing walk and it was really amazing because like, the moon was there and the stars were there and the ocean was there and the sand was there and I was there and he was there and like we got together and did it.*

Even though the character makes people laugh, the subject is serious. Like most of Whoopi’s comedy, it is both funny and sad. So why did she make it into a joke?

“I wanted to talk about a person’s right to make up her own mind,” Whoopi said of the routine. “Here’s a girl who’s speaking with all the affectations, all the slang of a teenager, but she’s saying serious things. And no one is really listening to her.

“And I thought, what if I talk about a kid in trouble? What

if I use the language of a teenager to talk about a teenager in trouble?

"So I did this [Valley girl sketch], and the response from people was amazing. They'd say 'Yes, that's my daughter; we had that problem, we went to talk to the nuns.' Or 'We went to talk to the rabbi.' And suddenly I realized that the whole sketch was about what happens when our children are in trouble. What happens when there is no help at home, when the parent has thrown the child out? Worse, what happens when there's no help from the places we have taught our children to *go* for help?

"What happens is that they take the problem upon themselves, and suddenly it's not so funny anymore."

As Whoopi would later discover, these trying events made her stronger. Her comedy became funnier. Her writing became more concise.

Her life took a turn for the better, too. Whoopi's daughter, Alex, had a healthy baby girl. And Whoopi was chosen for the role of Oda Mae Brown in *Ghost*.

Making the Political Personal

I believe that the things I talk about—which can get pretty dicey in places—are really God-driven, because they're all about taking real problems and using them to make the world a better place to live. My work is very spiritual. God and I are buds! I sit on God's shoulder; I tell God bad jokes. . . .

—Whoopi Goldberg

Whoopi Goldberg creates characters that many would consider out of the mainstream. Some are disabled. Some are in trouble with drugs. Some are homeless, others are wealthy. Some are wise, others are selfish and immature.

One thing binds them, however: Each one of Whoopi's characters faces great difficulty and in his or her own way finds a way to confront that difficulty. Sometimes it is not the right way, but it is all they know. And along the way, Whoopi strives to teach them compassion—or learn compassion from them.

Whoopi serves dinner at a homeless shelter.

Whoopi clowns around with some pals at a benefit for the Starlight Foundation.

This is quite deliberate. Having encountered hard times herself, Whoopi wants to use her art as a way of letting children know that there is a way to find solutions to life's problems, but it requires far more thought than simply saying no to drugs. It means thinking about one's family or one's history. It means thinking about one's personal strengths and weaknesses.

Because for Whoopi, social causes and her own comedy cannot be separate.

For example, as one who once lived on welfare and struggled to pay rent and food bills, Whoopi now helps the homeless. The HBO "Comic Relief" benefit, which Whoopi hosts, is in its sixth year. As many know, "Comic Relief" is a comedy show in which comedians donate performances to paying audiences. In turn, their money funds programs to help the homeless.

Said Whoopi, "It's our way of saying to the homeless 'Maybe the government doesn't care, but we care.'"

Another cause Whoopi supports is the fight against drugs. "Just Say No" isn't Whoopi's slogan, however. Whoopi is more direct. In addition to doing antidrug public-service announcements, Whoopi tries to weave her antidrug sentiments into her art.

For example, when planning her new late-night talk show, Whoopi said she was going to pay close attention to the show's advertisements so they might reflect her personal feelings about social issues.

"Like what?" interviewers wondered.

"Like the responsible use of alcohol," she responded. To show them what she meant, Whoopi, a nondrinker, gave them her idea for the perfect beer commercial:

[There are guys and] girls on the beach, everybody's playing volleyball, and they all have Budweisers. I just walk through the scene and ask, "Who's the designated driver?" One of the guys raises his hand with a glass of water. And I say, "Carry on."

Most visibly, Whoopi is an advocate of helping persons with AIDS (Acquired Immunodeficiency Syndrome). She appeared in an ad for America Responds to AIDS that warns people to be careful not to contract HIV (human immunodeficiency virus), the virus that causes AIDS. While hosting the Grammy awards show in 1992, Whoopi wore a red ribbon. She explained the ribbon symbolized the need for AIDS awareness, after which she performed a short piece on that theme with jazz vocalist Bobby McFerrin.

The AIDS community is very happy with her work and has given her many awards. For example, in 1987 AIDS Project Los Angeles deemed her the Entertainment Buddy of the Year.

Whoopi has even taken on the National Endowment for the Arts. During a recent scandal, the NEA wanted to limit funding of artists—among them comedians—whose work they considered obscene.

Whoopi fought back, saying, "These people undermine my ability as an artist to do what I want to do, to say what I want to say." Even though the censors did not accuse her of obscenity, Whoopi stood up for those the NEA did criticize. She said, "When you [censor someone else], you're making it easy for them to stop *you*."

On a more personal level, Whoopi's social causes also extended to promoting racial harmony.

The way she does this is by examining her own black heritage in the context of her writing and performance.

The most obvious example of this is *The Color Purple*, based on a novel by Alice Walker, a famous black author. But did you know that before appearing in *The Color Purple*, Whoopi starred in a one-woman show in San Francisco as the legendary black comedian Moms Mabley? The show, which she also co-wrote, used the late comedian's original material.

Whoopi also holds rights to *Major Taylor*, by Andrew Richi, the tale of the first black American world champion in any sport. And she was recently on location in South Africa, shooting the motion-picture version of the musical *Serafina!*

The point of these and other black-positive shows is that they allow Whoopi to help others, black and white, to embrace cultural history.

For Whoopi, this means examining the bad as well as the good of their heritage.

In the Alan King interview, Whoopi confirmed that she received much criticism from black groups because some of her characters have drawn upon the poor images of black people

Whoopi enjoys a quiet moment.

portrayed over the years. Groups were angry because they did not want to perpetuate these images. But Whoopi thinks it is necessary to point out these characters as a way of showing how silly they are.

"The older you get, you begin to realize all the wrong information you got about your people when you were growing up," she said of black people. "But it's very important to remember all the negative characters, the Stepin' Fetchit characters, or the white actors who made themselves up in blackface. Because then it makes you realize that a lot of these black performers—very talented people—never got to play the big theaters, the white theaters.

"You also have to remember that these bad images were all black people were given. When you have a people who all they were given was buffoonery, or servitude, you get to the place where you say 'I want my kids to know there is more for them in the world.'

"To me, [recognizing this as a black woman] meant self-assurance."

And, it would seem, a certain power.

Whoopi has received many awards from the black community. The NAACP is one of her biggest fans, having awarded her its Image award in 1986, 1988, 1989, 1990, and 1991.

For Whoopi, attention to social causes has become a hallmark of her art. One gets the idea that talking about social issues is far less a crime than *not* talking about them.

Life As Whoopi Knows It

I'm from the projects. I became a movie star. It's a great thing that's happened to me.
                                        —Whoopi Goldberg

It is a steamy summer day. Whoopi is standing on a wooden dais at San Francisco's Comedy Day. She addresses a sunburned crowd: "I have to say thank you to San Francisco because before coming here nobody gave a hoot about me. It took people in San Francisco to say this chick is hot.

"So now I'm famous, I'm riding around in a red Porsche, and I just want to say thank you, and my welfare check I will pass out to everyone."

The crowd cheers.

Whoopi has always been grateful to those who've helped her achieve success. That is no secret.

What is surprising about this speech, however, is that in 1984—a year before *The Color Purple* and seven before

Whoopi's determination and ability to laugh at life have helped her make it to the top.

Ghost—Whoopi still had not reached the height of her fame.

This is just one example of Whoopi's eagerness to help or praise those who have helped her rise to the top. For example, in an industry where many comedians steal from one another, Whoopi gives credit to those who have helped her develop. Whoopi is the first to admit that she got the idea for her surfer girl character from another character by fellow comedian Taylor Negron. When the San Francisco comedy troupe she'd once joined as a budding comedian needed money for a recent project, Whoopi bankrolled the show. And when Irish comedian Billy Connolly opened his show in the United States, Whoopi was there to introduce him to American audiences.

While Whoopi spends much time at her home in California, she still keeps an apartment in Manhattan, not far from the Hudson Guild. It's not unusual to see Whoopi stop by and say hello to everyone, to play with the children of her old friends, to sign autographs.

Today Whoopi handles fame a little better than when she first hit it big. It is still difficult, however. When one interviewer asked her how she was handling fame, Whoopi said, "This isn't

Whoopi poses for a picture with friends and family.

how I thought it was gonna be. I thought [fame] would be hunky-dory. I thought I'd be able to take people on a wonderful adventure to places they'd never been, because I had the opportunity. And what it did was it drove terrible wedges between friends and myself."

She recently described herself as being "in a state of flux" as she tries to face this problem of balancing the aims of her career with the aims of her personal life.

But whether she does more or less comedy in the future, one thing is sure: The *nature* of Whoopi's comedy will never change.

It will always be challenging and, at the same time, responsible.

Why? Because in the facts of her life, Whoopi has always been honest. For example, Whoopi neither denies nor celebrates her drug use. Instead she talks about her addiction, in the hope that others will not start taking drugs. She does so, she says, because she wants to be a responsible artist and citizen.

Take her character Fontaine, the ex-junkie.

When Whoopi first created the character, Fontaine was using drugs. "But then I started getting all these fan letters from 10- and 11-year-old kids who were allowed to watch my work and who really loved him. And I thought, man, if they love him that much, I'm going to have to clean him up. I don't want people or children thinking that it's okay to be a junkie."

Whoopi, as his creator, could do anything with him.

She changed Fontaine. As she did with herself when she was a teenager, she sent Fontaine to the rehabilitation center. She sent him to the Betty Ford clinic.

It must have worked: Her performance of Fontaine (post-Betty Ford) was nominated for a Grammy.

These days Whoopi can pretty much write her own ticket. In 1992, for example, Whoopi began the year by making two movies and watching the release of a third. One was *Sister Act*, a comedy about a woman who moves to a convent to escape hoods. The second was *Change of Heart* with Ted Danson.

These and other projects confirm that Whoopi is a full-fledged movie star.

And, not surprisingly, she is rumored to be as testy as a typical movie star. But if you watch her interviews very carefully, you can still see the little girl who longs to be famous. You can see the girl who once said, in an amazed whisper, "I became a movie star. *Me!*"

INDEX

ABOUT THE AUTHOR

Mary Agnes Adams is a writer, editor, and novelist who lives in Brooklyn, New York. In the past she's written about photography, rap music, television, and literature. When she's not in the reading room of the New York Public Library, she likes to frequent comedy and dance clubs.